Environmental Economy and Futuristic Solutions

WASTE MANAGEMENT AND ECONOMY

SHUBHANG DIXIT KULDEEP DHAKAR

pencil

ISBN 978-93-5667-006-8

Published in India 2022 by Pencil

A brand of
One Point Six Technologies Pvt. Ltd.
123, Building J2, Shram Seva Premises,
Wadala Truck Terminal, Wadala (E)
Mumbai 400037, Maharashtra, INDIA
E connect@thepencilapp.com
W www.thepencilapp.com

Author biography

Shubhang Dixit is social activist, author, founder and president of several Organisations, environment activist.
He is also working for environment education and awareness of the society even that can be seen in his writing as well.

Kuldeep Dhakar is social worker, author, Environment thinker; he worked as key member and co-founder in several organisations.
He is working for health and environment awareness in rural and slum areas.

CONTENTS

WASTE MANAGEMENT AND ECONOMY

Index

Environmental Economy and structure

The environmental economy is the need of today and the solution for generations.

But what exactly is an Environmental Economy?
An economy where natural resources are used for living is called the Environmental economy.
Every individual or person needs money for living and for that they choose a medium to earn money but there's a dependency on resources which are not environment friendly so people must switch to an environmental economy.
So that environment will be the source of economy.
By making the environmental economy we can minimize exploitation of the environment and that is the key to sustainable development as well.
To make this plan work each class of society needs to step up and play their roles,

For example, government, non-government organizations, cooperative organizations, capitalists and the general public should work together by creating an environmental platform and playing their roles.
To Encouragement the environmental economy environmental programmes should be introduced in a certain manner:
the gardening programme (kitchen garden)
rooftop gardens
public gardens
In every public garden, there should be a nursery for selling plants so that way employment opportunities will be generated and the caretaker can maintain the garden or bear the expenses of the garden.
Small nurseries are classified in three ways-:
First – oxygen plants
Second – medicinal plants

Third - floral plants

Roles of entities and individuals –

Governmental bodies - Allocation of land, subsidize environmental business, develop special environmental zones (environmental institutions, nationalised nursery with garden) at every district 7% GDP expenditure (environmental education, generate employment, sanitation environment tourism and pollution control)

Non- governmental organization –

Work for social environmental awareness, NGOs will play a part in awareness of the governmental project on the environment and start an institution for education or training or research programmes with public funds.

COOPERATIVE ORGANIZATION for the environment – THE cooperative organization for the environment is an organization where small; businessmen, teachers, students, and people from rural and urban areas are working together for environmental benefits.

Investment by the Capitalist or industrialist-

Invest capital for the environment to build environmental industries, and develop environmental zones as per the need of the area (if some place or area is low oxygen zone then develop that area by planting oxygen plants.

Cottage industry – this is an industry known as small scale industry in the environment sector and needs to promote such kind of industry for environmental benefits by developing environment-friendly products-

Examples – soil products, leave bags, bamboo sticks products, natural fertilizers etc.

Banking infrastructure for the environment – providing loans to environment cottage industries and other enExamplesvironmental industries, environmental bonds, mutual funds,

Industrial Environmental Regulatory body for the multi-national company (IERB)

Structure of commission -

In this commission, there should be five members in penal

Tenure of the members for five years.

Constitute a committee by every country's government or state

ELIGIBILITY CRITERIA–

FIRST MEMBER (ADVOCATE)

SECOND MEMBER (A PERSON FROM THE COMPANY)

THIRD MEMBER (ENVIRONMENTAL ACTIVIST)

FOURTH MEMBER (AUDITOR)

FIFTH MEMBER (ECONOMIST)

WORK AREA OF COMMISSION –

Commission will regulate and monitor whether the fund invested or expended, by the company is for environmental growth or not.

The company must Invest 7% of their wealth or profit in environmental businesses.

Commission will publicise the report and submit it to the Central government or take necessary actions for environmental benefits as per the requirement of the situation.

This can be applied nationally, internationally or state-wise as well

Roles of United Nations (UN) (international, national or state)

· Build an International court of environment.

· Build an International Constitution for the environment.

· Build environmental educational institutions and research

centres (environment-course – law, economics, history, traditional nature-based technology, world gardening training programme, etc.).

· International, national or state bank for the environment (applies to all international, national or state).

Provide a Common forum for environmental discussion to the world's NGOs or environmental activists.

Build an institution for water crisis and water conservation or water treatment.

Build an International platform for farmers where they can get a training programme to grow a crop in difficult conditions or exchange and grow crops from other countries.

the Environment is the only thing which unites the world. Every person can affect it from any kind of careless behaviour towards the environment or exploitation of the environment by carbon emissions or polluting environmental resources.

Why do we need an environment-based economy?

For 500 years, humans have exploited the environment for their greediness & to fulfil their blind ambitions. Now it's time to understand the serious problem we are facing at this point which is climate change. To save this planet, we need to work sustainably by making an environment-based economy or making an environmental economy.

INSTITUTIONALIZATION OF WASTE MANAGEMENT AND MAKING IT ENVIRONMENTAL ECONOMY

Plastic Waste management

It is now to rethink and human needs to change the perspective of seeing waste as a waste it can be turned into an economy too.

There is only one way to make it possible by developing such industries which can work on waste and turn the waste into different forms of usable materials.

Plastic substances are very dangerous to the environment as we all know humans are very dependent on plastic products because our dependency on the consumption of plastic is increasing day by day very rapidly.

In 2019 global plastic production was 368 million metric tons which was an increase of 100 million metric tons comparatively from the year 2010 this should be a matter of concern for humans and the entire ecosystem, but the nations like china and America are producing highly plastic products their production and profit of market is depending on plastic products.

Market and profits of nations -

In 2020 global market value of plastic waste was 593 billion US dollars approximately and which is an estimated 367 million metric tons a few agencies predicted that by the end of 2050 the production would be approximately 590 million metric tons this is forecast when we were pushing to minimize the use of plastic.

China plastic market –

China is the biggest market for plastic production in the world and china has a 32% hold on global plastic material production also china is the largest exporter of plastic products.

Consumption of plastic in china

China has a high volume of plastic consumption and it was almost 91 million metric tons the rate of consumption is increasing day by day china has the highest population in the world and because of that china has the largest number of consumers of plastic.

Consumption of plastic in the United States of America

Ithe n U.S as to data from 2016, America is the second largest plastic-consuming country in the world and the amount of plastic used is 42 million metric tons but when we see per capita wise plastic consumption per person uses 129 kg.

the Total number of plastic used by America and china is approximately 36% of world consumption and releases plastic waste into the environment.

Consumption of plastic in Europe and the discovery

Plastic was first introduced to the mass population by Phillips Petroleum, J. Paul Hogan and Robert Banks in 1951 this pioneering discovery led to large–scale commercial productions of polypropylene by the Italian firm Montecatini from 1957 onwards.

Chronological development of plastic

Europe and America were the discovery centre of polypropylene, The first synthetic polymer was invented in 1869 by john Wesley Hyatt, the reason discovery took place was because a New York firm offered ten thousand US dollars for finding substitutes of natural materials like – wood, metal, horn, stone, ivory and in replacement of these materials synthetic polymer (celluloid) has taken the place.

In 1907 Leo Baekeland discovered Bakelite the first fully synthetic plastic that contained no molecules found in nature.

At the time of the Second World War, the USA expanded the plastic industry for military success on the war front, but after 75 years of this industry, we have seen disasters impact plastic into the environment.

"Baekeland" was searching for a substitution for a natural electrical insulator to complete or fulfil the need for rapid electrification of the United States.

But in the year of early 1990s the problems from plastics that came out could be seen in the environment after that a few countries started banning plastic from their nations and now in 2022, it is the biggest problem for the planet.

As per waste releases to the environment, they are highly responsible for pollution even though they are economical competent in waste management but these countries are not taking responsibility for the role they should have played by these countries.

Consumption of plastic in low-Middle-income countries

This is not only the problem as we all know plastic takes 400 years or sometimes more than that to decompose the problem with these countries middle income countries have not very economically competent in the recycling of plastic Products because south Asian, African, and Latin American countries are already facing many financial issues.

But other European and developed countries using to middle-income countries as dumping spaces, they throw their waste to countries like –

African country Ghana dumping grounds:

Agbogbloshie is a nickname for a commercial district on

the korle lagoon of the Odaw River, near the centre of Accra, Ghana's capital city in the greater Ghana region near the slum called "old Fadama", the Agbogbloshie site became known as a destination for externally generated automobile and electronic scrap collected from most of the western countries.

In 2019 was collected almost 50 million tons but the big concern is more than that only 20% of waste gets recycled if the condition will not be changing in future years then the E-waste will be 100 million tons by 2050.

Ghana has facing many issues because of the dumped waste and the 10 thousand or more informal workers work there to collect scrap to recycle this way they get money.

But the problem apart from collected scrap, the workers are facing health issues working in that dumping ground such as –skin problems and respiratory illnesses even also the problem with these workers now.

According to the United Nations environment programme, 85 Percentage of the e-waste is dumped in Ghana and other parts of West Africa.

Latin American and Caribbean countries dumping grounds:

The United States and European companies dump millions of tontons toxic waste in Latin American and Caribbean countries every year, dropping poisonous material in Brazil, Mexico, Argentina and other countries.

Even though they continue to use these countries as dumping spots the developed nations offer them a loan, and projects to build schools, hospitals and roads because dumping yard situations are getting worst and pollution is increasing day by day.

Asian countries dumping grounds:
75% of the world's exported waste ends up in Asia.
China was the main importer country of plastic waste before 2017, when the ban was not imposed by china, the annual imports of plastic waste reached 8.88 million tons, with as much as 70% buried or even mismanaged, triggering problems there. To avoid this situation china imposed a new bill called prohibition of foreign garbage imports: the reform plan on waste import management, this bill aimed to ban 24 types of solid waste including plastic.
Before the ban china used to import approximate 55% of the world's plastic waste.
After the plastic ban by china, the countries like America and western countries were looking for a dumping place, so they started dumping their waste in south-east Asian countries: Such as Malaysia, Indonesia, the Philippines etc.
Indian's dumping grounds:
India is a country that generates 62 million tons per year and every five years generation of waste gets doubles in their figures.
Data By the environment ministry
In 2015-16 countries produced 1.5 million tons of plastic waste in 2019-20 more than 3.4 million tons of plastic were generated in India with an average annual increase of 21.8per cent.
With the increasing population the s and urbanization in India, waste management has become a major challenge, especially in the urban setup.
Over the years, there has been a stark increase in the quantity of waste generated, and it is also expected to increase in the coming years as per the government

estimated that reached 165 million tons in 2031 which the challenges to the environmental wealth of the country.

Why E-waste is a concern:

This is the waste where the electronic used products at the end of useful life than throughout in form of E-waste and waste releases the most poisonous elements like – beryllium, cadmium, mercury and lead etc.

Which causes serious environmental risks to soil, water, and air even though it's more dangerous for humans.

Common e-waste Items:

Such as - Home appliances, communications and information technology, entertainment devices, electronic utilities and medical equipment etc.

The main reason for increasing waste that is new technologies are taking place every day so the old technologies are getting pointless to people so every person is looking for new phones and other stuff and throwing out their old ones.

A Problem from E-waste:

E-Waste is a bigger problem than any other solid waste the reason it is a combination of plastic and other toxic materials.

World's biggest major waste landfills:

Las Vegas (USA)

The 2200 –acre area apex regional landfill in Las Vegas daily receives about 9000 tons of municipal solid waste, though it can handle up to 15 thousand tons daily. The landfill is the biggest in the USA.

Bordo Poniente(Mexico)

The acre landfills in Mexico. The City received 12 thousand of the 15 thousand tons of waste generated in the city daily and an estimated 70 million tons of waste deposited there which is a big concern for the environmental ecosystem.

Leogang (China)

At 892 acres in area and piled 20 meters high, the Leogang landfill in Shanghai city is one of the biggest in Asia. It receives up to 10 thousand tons of municipal solid waste.

Malagrotta (Italy)

The 618 – acres of Malagrotta landfill in Rome, Italy has a holding capacity of 60 million tons. It receives between 4500 and 5000 tons of waste per day. It is one of the biggest municipal solid waste facilities in Europe.

Puente Hills (USA)

The Landfill was opened in 1957 as the privately owned San Gabriel Valley dump and until it was not closed 130 million tons of loss angel municipal waste had been dumped.

Sudokwon (South Korea)

It is South Korea's largest landfill and receives 18,000 to 20,000 tons of waste daily from the capital city of South Korea.

Delhi landfills (India)

The city of New Delhi generates about 9200 tons of municipal solid waste daily according to the municipal council Delhi.

This waste is deposited in the Narelabawana, Bawana, Bhalswa Okhla, and Gaazipur landfills, which have a combined acreage of 316. Except for Narela Bawana, a new landfill, the others have been exhausted waste continues being dumped upon them.

Deonar landfills (India)

Annually, India generates 60 million tons of waste which 2.7 million tons are generated in Mumbai city alone, according to the central pollution control board data of 2014.

Waste new territories (Hong Kong)

On daily Basics, since 2007 Hong Kong has generated over 13000 tonnes of municipal solid waste from its businesses, households, and industries combined, according to the environmental protection department.

Xinfeng china

Guangzhou is china's largest city, with a population of about 14 million people. On any given day, the city generates over 8 thousand tons of waste, with 3800 tons coming from households in the rest from institutions this landfill is one of the largest in Asia, according to Bio-cycle global, and was built at a cost of dollar 100 million US dollar and its disposal capacity are 1.5765 million tons.

Fact, these are a major concern but apart from this there are many areas covered by landfill in small cities and remote areas of countries and the total number of landfills is almost 100,000 approximately.

Because of that, there are so many problems arising in the environment and direct effects are seen.

A Problem from landfills in human lives & environmental –

Underground Water

Landfills and industrial waste are the biggest reason for pollution contaminated in groundwater the most impact can see in urban areas, especially in metro cities because of rapid urbanisation and pollutions growth so the human and E-waste are also increasing.

Global annual waste is generating almost 2.01 billion tons in the world by end of 2050 waste will increase by 3.4 billion tons.

Drinking water and surface water are 1.5 km away from the landfill area of Ghana during the season of rain, many types of gases flow with rainy water and contaminant the Groundwater and surface water, because of contamination many health issues can be seen in populated areas.
Contaminated elements are known as methane, gasoline, arsenic, lead, etc.
Heavy Metals
Cd, Cr, Cu, Fe, Ni, Pv, Fe and Zn etc.
Health issues
The health issue can be seen in the human body because of contamination of groundwater by dumping waste onto landfills.
Such as-
Diarrhoea, Cholera, Dysentery, Hepatitis A, typhoid, Polio etc.

At present two million tons of trash people produced each year globally this is the data based on weight measured and on the other hand, more than 70% of the waste produced from urban areas, especially the metro cities is very much responsible for that.
Landfill area of trash will be just double by 2050 from now, the reason for increasing waste every day, as we see from a broader perspective area covered by landfills almost 0.5 - 1% of the total world's urban area and this issue will be the biggest problem if we don't find any solutions for it so landfills will increase up to almost 2-2.5% total world's urban land area.
Air pollution from solid waste (landfills)
There are many reasons for greenhouse gases but one of the impacts of greenhouse gases due to landfills and solid waste has been seen.

As - carbon-di-oxide (Co2), methane (CH4), and Chloro Fluoro Carbon (CFC) are gasses emitted into the atmosphere which cause pollution and climate change. Almost 20% of greenhouse gases are produced by burning waste in landfills, even in some cases, small chunks are burned at the household level in every residential area this is the primary source of methane gas.

Methane impacts the environment due to the burning of landfills and solid waste

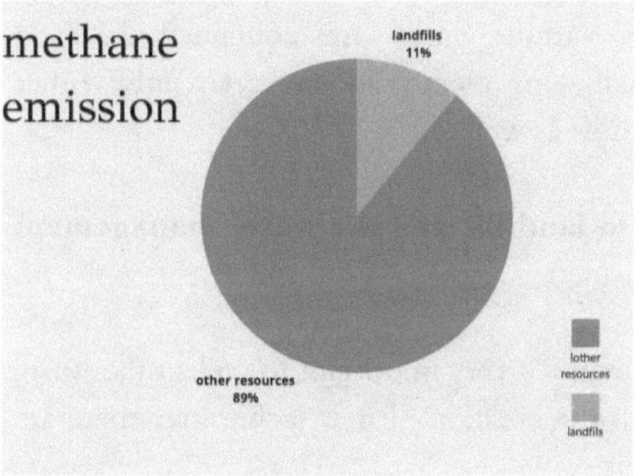

methane emission chart

Anthropogenic methane emission charts

The Earth's atmospheric concentration already has increased by 150% since 1750 and it accounts for 20% of the total radiative forcing from the entire long-lived and globally mixed greenhouse gasses but the main source of releasing methane is landfill, which is causing global warming.

Methane is more than 25 times as vigorous as carbon dioxide.

Methane produces a high level of heat in the Atmosphere.

USA, CHINA, INDIA, NIGERIA, MEXICO, BRAZIL,

INDONESIA AND RUSSIA are responsible for nearly half of the world's total methane emissions and globally landfills are responsible for 11% of total methane emissions in the world.

The source of methane emission in America (USA)

Landfills are the third biggest cause of methane emission which is 14.5% of total methane emission in America is only from anthropogenic, landfill releases many gases but 50% only methane gas released from landfills and the mixture of other gases are also hazardous such as – carbon dioxide 40 %, nitrogen, ammonia, sulphides, hydrogen including other various gases are contained 10% in landfills, the same problem can be seen into other developed countries as well.

The solutions to landfills and the waste management (model)

Waste management: it's very important to collect the waste scientifically with the creation of new technology there are four ways to do it.

Collection->Transportation-> Recycle ground -> energy generation station

Collection

Collection of waste is an important factor in the waste management process, but more than 25 % of the produced waste is not even collected, it doesn't mean it should be collect in landfills. The Collection of waste must be directly collected to recycling grounds.

What is recycling grounds?

Recycling grounds are different from dumping grounds (landfills). In the recycling grounds, there should be a recycling plant and mandatorily the waste must be completely recycled within two months from the date when waste is collected by the agency in the recycling grounds, the reason for two month time period of recycling the waste because the waste starts decomposing and resealing hazardous gases after this period and after time situations gets worst day by day for the environment.

Transportation

Transportation is the key factor in garbage or waste management, when the agencies transport the waste by ships and other transportation resources it costs billions of dollars to the government or their agencies.

When we see some data it says 70% of total waste management, it's spends only on their transportation to other countries and in the country as well.

Waste can be managed by reducing the cost of transportation and developing recycling grounds at regional levels, in every region of cities like Gwalior produce waste approximately 300 tonnes per day if we talk about Delhi figure is quite big it's more than 11 thousand tonnes per day so the only solution is to build recycling and waste to Energy plants in every regional level (at least every 700 tonnes per day production) and sub-station plants of recycling project should be at (every 300 tonnes per day production) that can be called as energy generation station.

What are energy generation stations?

Energy is an essential part of the life process for the entire world or universe it is a crucial part of the human life circle every day such - as electricity and fuels (petrol, diesel, gas, coal, etc.)

Energy generation station

It is an energy-producing from the waste and final stage for disposable waste into an energy form, that energy will help people in their daily life circle.

In the world, waste is only processed or recycled by 9% of total produced waste and that is not a good number when we talk about other Asian countries like India production of waste is 277.1 million tonnes per day and landfills are more than 4000 if we think about the area of landfills it captures approximately 200,000 acres that are when we take

50 acres in an average per dumping ground (landfills) site area this problem has the only solution that is the creation of energy stations in every district of the country.

How much energy we can produce from the waste?

Every leading country is finding a way to deal with a problem like waste restoration or converting waste into usable energy.

Model of the countries for converting waste into energy

Sweden

Sweden country is known for global sustainable waste management and Recycling is part of Swedish tradition, they recycle, reuse and change waste to energy, Sweden almost recycles 99% of total waste generation and 1% of waste only goes to landfills, Sweden generates 52% of energy by the garbage and rest of waste are used as ash in construction of a building and other activities in process of recycling.

The country generates electricity from garbage for two fifty lakh households and heat provided 10 lakh households

Through this process, Sweden reduced its carbon dioxide emission by 2.2 million tonnes annually.

Denmark

Denmark is the biggest user of district heating in Europe now country has shifted to waste-based energy generation from fossil energy reducing greenhouse and carbon emissions.

Demark has awareness of public funding and investment in the waste incineration sector that helps to recycle or waste treat almost 68% of total waste.

United States of America

The Technology of energy generation from garbage began in

1960 seems very problematic at first but after a while, the local leadership also took initiative for this technology

of energy production, after the success of some projects, the federal government started a rebate system to attract private capital investment in the industry which were developing at the time of 1975 but from 1995 to 2014 there was not any new projects or development in the industry due to hitch by communities and transportation of solid waste was the reason as well but one other reason was that the local living people were opposing too apart from some communities because dumping into landfills was easier or cheaper than transporting waste to energy (WTE) facilities centre.

Recently Supreme Court of the US has given a verdict "Supreme Court decision on flow control has restored the ability of communities to enact flow control ordinances and enable them to direct their wastes to WTE facilities"

That promotes waste to facility centres, and waste to energy industries ad the total number of facilities centres 87 are in America, about 7% of the nation's MSW or about 90,000 tons per day this generates 2700 megawatts of electricity and that fulfils the electricity needs of 2 million homes.

Now America is planning to reduce plastic waste into useable fuel, the American chemistry council estimated that the plastic-to-fuel facility would create almost 40,000 jobs and the economic profit is the surplus for the American economy.

The estimated economical profit would be almost $9 billion in plastic to fuel industries for America, making globally or understanding the potential of this industry can be huge.

The plastic to diesel

The chemist from the University of California, Irvine (UC) in the collaboration with researchers from the shanghai institute of organic chemistry has found there is a technique or method that allows to dissolving of the bonds of polyethene plastic to create petroleum and other fuel products.

There is certain other technique to turn plastic into other fuel like crude oil and plastic into sulphur as fuel.

China

China is the world's second-largest economy because of its larger GDP there are many developed and developing sectors that can be seen in the country and the vividness of the success is hiding many dark truths about China.

In the present scenario, China is the largest solid waste producer and carbon emitter country in the world, it left behind the US in 2004 for municipal solid waste production, but china tries to minimize its waste and converting into energy for china's households.

Many countries are establishing plants for a waste-to-energy generation but China is one of the leading countries in the world, the Luganzen plant in Shanghai China is one of the largest waste-to-energy (WTE) plants in the world and its electricity generation capacity is 60,000 kilowatts that burns 1 million tons annually.

China is one of the largest markets of waste to energy and china installed almost 400 centres in 2018, China is planning to double the capacity of incineration and the total capacity of burning 54% of municipal solid waste.

China has developed the largest WTE plant in the world with a capacity of 5,000 tons of waste burning per day and electricity generating for 20 million people, country already has more than 300 WTE operational Plant.

This increased annual capacity by 26% over the last five years, which shows the growth rate of China is almost 7 times more than OECD countries.

These are the leading countries and using waste or trash as reusable energy this is the perfect model or example for the other countries as well.

Waste can be turned into usable fuel

Road construction

Road construction is the key medium for transportation. The Total road network is constructed in the world almost 64,285,009 km and the biggest network of the road is considered the United States which has almost 9703479 km even other countries have the biggest road network in the world – India, China, Russia, Brazil some of these nations are working very fast in the road construction, these countries are constructing collectively lakhs of a kilometre in every year but it is time to shift by using plastic and other waste for road construction.

Now we can use plastic in road construction and the durability of the plastic road will be longer than the traditional way of road construction.

The plastic roads are composites of plastic with some other materials and it minimizes human-produced plastic waste.

There are two kinds of plastic roads.

The first type of plastic road is made of modular, hollow and prefabricated road elements made from waste consumer plastic.

The way of constructing roads by Asphalt mix with waste plastic products incorporated into the asphalt mix.

Plastic can be processed in two ways dry and wet process.

Dry process

It should be clean first and cut into 1.18mm to 4.36mm in the shedding machine, the PVC should be eliminated from the plastic waste in the cleaning process.

The temperature needed to be 165*C approximately and the bitumen mixture heated to an extent of 160*C

Wet process

The plastic is collected 60-micron size mix with hot bitumen at 160*C to 170*C temperature, At the constant temperature, the mixture is stirred manually for about 20-30 minutes.

Many countries are using plastic to construct their roads.

India

Chennai was the first city in India who has adopted plastic road construction technology for building the plastic road very first time in the world.

Chennai build 1000km of plastic roads in 2004, it was constructed in Dharmapuri district as per the guidelines of the chief minister's office at that time then the major municipality in India experimented with the same technology in cities like Pune, Delhi, Lucknow, Surat, Mumbai, Indore etc.

In 2011 Chennai has used plastic near about 1600 tonnes of waste to construct a road of 1,035 kilometres in length.

The history of plastic road

Plastic is the biggest concern in the world and many countries try to recycle or reuse it in different ways but India was the first country that developed the method of using plastic in road construction such a type of road was called a plastic road and it was a great revolution for the world.

The plastic roads helped to reuse the plastic waste because millions of tonnes can be transformed waste plastic into usable plastic.

Rajagopalan vasudevan

He is an Indian scientist who developed the method to reuse plastic waste to construct better, more durable and very cost-effective roads, roads were more resistant to damages caused by water during rains.

Rajagopalan Vasudevan invented it in 2001 and the patent was held by the Thiagarajar College of Engineering in 2006. At present, there are so many countries that have used technology for road building from plastic waste such as Netherland, Australia, Indonesia, India, Indonesia, the United States and the United Kingdom.

Now at the world's forum, other countries are trying to create or innovate a new model which is suitable for their countries and it could help to reduce plastic waste.

Bricks

Bricks are so commonly used for construction purposes but now 80 % of bricks are produced in India and some other developing countries are fired clay bricks (red clay bricks).

These bricks are produced from the fired clay burning in a kiln, there are some other kinds of bricks fly Ash, sand lime gypsum and cement. The fire clay bricks industries and such industries of bricks are a concern for the environment the large number of production of clay bricks are major environmental footprint.

The bricks industries are the fifth largest consumer of coal in the country that's why the bricks industries rerelease huge sources of particulate matter emissions and are also one of the largest carbon emitters of carbon dioxide and black carbon.

The only way to reduce and minimize this problem is by using plastic waste to build bricks, In India and other countries release a high amount of plastic in the households area and consumption of plastic are mainly seen in areas like Railway station, Bus stand and other crowded places.

The reason behind this is very simple people are so dependent on plastic bottles for their drinking requirements the water bottles and the plastic of the bottles are not decomposed in the environment.

The problem is more severe in the rainy season because plastic contaminates the soil and reaches Rivers, lakes and other water resources and flows with the rivers even it causes land pollution, Air pollution and Water pollution.

This is one of the reasons for causes of Malaria, dengue, plague and Ret bite fever to rescue people from this problem the government and society need to initiate using plastic composite bricks in construction.

Rural Economy development

Home (house) Building- House is a basic need for humans but is not easy to build a home for people who come from a financial weaker background because the construction of a house is very costly. Financial weaker sections of society depended on the government for their basic needs like food, health facilities and residential facilities in countries in Asia and Africa.

In India poverty rate is estimated at 21.9% which is almost 270 million it means every fifth Indian life below the poverty line and 17% of the urban population lives in the slums which are roughly 1.37 Cr. Households, this problem is quite big when we see it in the world.

In some cities in the developing world slum residents make up more than half of the population so often they are facing an issue of inadequate shelter, clean water, sanitation, education or healthcare.

A glimpse at the world's five biggest slums

Khayelitsha Cape Town South Africa (population 400,000)

Kibera, Nairobi, Kenya (population 700,000)

Ciudad Neza, Mexico City, Mexico (1.2 million)

Dharavi, Mumbai, India (population 10,00000)

Orange town, Karachi, Pakistan(2.4 million)

In the slum areas, shelter is not just a difficult task when we understand the seriousness of the problem even if they have trouble with toilets it causes diseases such as diarrhoea, Hepatitis and other chronic diseases.

The United Nations Human Settlements program reports an estimated 1.6 billion people around the world living in inadequate housing and over 100 million people with no housing at all.

What can be the eco-friendly solution for those slum areas?

The all-new concept of recycling plastic and building a home made of plastic is one of a solution to plastic and house crises too. This concept will be a milestone for those people who suffer from homelessness and also an eco-friendly solution for the environment.

"One man's trash is another man's treasure" this aphorism is a truth of today's world.

The recycled plastic mixed with sand creates plastic bricks even recycling material rubber is helpful in home building for those who are in need.

What is the Advantage of this concept?

In this concept of house building plastic and old tires, the plastic entire goes to the factory and by the processing of plastic and melting of a tire with few additives finally, it turns into beams, pillars and blocks.

These pillars, beams and blocks can be assembled within a week by less than five people, this construction is earthquake resistant, easy to maintain and importantly cost-efficient this way the person can save lots of money or it will cost up to 10,000 dollars.

It can be more beneficial for rural areas as well, the government can take the initiative to build schools, warehouses and primary health care centres at the primary level.

Waste management and recycling of glass and rubber
Glass

Recycling glass is important but for a long, while only plastic had all the attention it does not mean the glass is not getting recycled but it is on a very small scale of recycling at the present.

As you all know glass takes more than 4,000 years to 5,000 years to decompose in the environment, it takes ten times longer period to decompose than plastic this is the longest period of decomposition.

Some examples of common waste and the degradation period in nature:

Cigar butts: 1-2 years

Chewing gums: 5 years

Rubber: 50-70 years

Soda cane: 200-500 years

Plastics: 500 years

This period of decomposition like waste leads to numerous problems.

Glass specifically causes common or hazardous risks to an environment like water contamination, soil and the entire ecosystem too.

The population are increasing every single day and the consumption of glasses is twice bigger in figures, the number of increasing glass production is approximately 130 million tonnes worldwide annually as per data from the pre-covid-19 pandemic 2018, which increased by the growth rate of 4.1%.

The current growth rate of America, china and a few other countries has quite higher so the consumption rate of glass is high as well; the larger volume of 63 million tonnes or 48% is accounted for container glass, 54 million tonnes or 42% are accounted for construction, window glass, car glass, the 5% consumption for tableware and the 5% for different glass products.

The five biggest glass exporters are mainland China, Germany, the United States of America, France and Hong Kong. In 2021 these countries were the Major exporters, the overall generation was 48% of glass even if we talk about material plus glassware products and these countries had the highest figure in the world.

The glasses exported to these countries

Glass fibres, glass wool

The glass container including the bottles pot

Tampered and the laminated safety glasses

Sheet glass, tableware, kitchenware and decorative items.

Glass mirrors

Laboratory or pharmaceutical glasses

The countries are doing by global trade (export) of glass and the profit estimated by all that 86.8 billion US dollars in 2021, this growth rate lifting Almost by 18% per year.

Past situations and the Historical development of glass:

The history of glass creation is known from 3,500 -4,000 years back in Mesopotamia or some historian claims may be in Egypt. By the 15th century BCE occurring in western Asia, Crete, and Egypt the glass was a magical object at that time for those who had seen the first time and they were surprised to see that it was a luxury material only used by 1% to 2% of the elite society such as king not used by common people as present time.

The first Persian glass had seen in 1600 BCE and discovered during the exploration of Dinkhah Tepe in Iranian.

In India the glass first time found at Harappa dating to 1700 BCE, this is the first evidence of glass in South Asia. The glass was found in different colours later 600 to 300 BCE and displays common colours.

China was the first evidence of glass in the Warring States period at 475-221 BCE; they were using it for arts and crafts glass made a place in their culture to replace ceramics and metals.

Glass developed in China later than in Mesopotamia, Egypt and India.

Europe

First time in Europe glass object was found on the island of Torcello near Venice at the time of the Roman Empire which was nearly the 7th to 8th century but a flourishing glass industry developed at the end of the 13th century when Venice became a major glass-making centre. In the period of the 15th century, experts believe the object's major producer was Venice.

Development of glass at the time of the colonial era

The colonial era was a dark period for the world stain cannot be removed till now but the colonial era was the golden period for global trade, new techniques were developed for adding lead oxide to molten glass this improved appearance of the glass and because of it the process of making glass improved and it reaches to the world.

So the rich people showed a lot of interest in glass and glass-made products and even started using them in their palaces, their homes and other luxurious items as well.

The first example of the Crystal palace in 1851 was built by Joseph Paxton a house that used glass as a building material the house was the Great Exhibition Paxton's revolutionary new building inspired the public to use glass as a material for domestic and horticulture architecture.

The company adopted the cylindrical method to produce glass sheets with the expertise of Gorges Bontemps a famous French glass maker.

James Hartley introduced rolled plat method in 1847.

An early advance in automating glass manufacturing was patented in 1848 by the engineer Henry Bessemer.

The first mechanical method for drawing window glass in the US was licensed in the UK by Pilkington from 1910 onwards the method was called the machine draft technique invented by the US.

In 1938, the Polish plate process was improved by Pilkington which incorporated a double grinding process to give improve the quality of the finishing of the glass work.

In 1953 and 1957 Sir Alastair Pilkington and Kenneth Bickerstaff of the UK discovered the technology of float glass.

The full profitability of float glass was achieved in 1960.

Now in the 21st century the, profit of glass has increased and the figures for profit are improving by every single day.

The profit generated by the countries from exportation:

China: 21.6 billion US$(24% highest profit by export)
Germany: US$7.8 billion (9%)
United States: US$5.6 billion (6.5%)
France: US$3.5 billion (4%)
Hong Kong: US$3.26 billion (3.8%)
Japan: US$3.21 billion (3.7%)
Italy: US$3 billion (3.5%)
Poland: US$2.7 billion (3.1%)
Belgium : US$2.51 billion (2.9%)
South Korea: US$2.2 billion (20.5%)

The world's giant economies and their expenditure

China

China is one of the leading Economies of the world; they invested in Research and development (R&D) almost 2% of the GDP size of china's economy, 4.22% in education, on military budget china hike their budget by 7.1 % from previous years total sending of by the China 230 billion US dollar and on pollution control just 1.15% of the total share of GDP. The GDP size of the second highest is about 14.72 trillion.

UNITED STATES OF AMERICA

The United State of America is highly developed and wealthy with its market, it is the world's largest nominal GDP.

The United States has the second largest purchasing power after china; the USA is the most technologically powerful and innovative economy.

The USA has left behind many countries in technology such as artificial intelligence, computers, pharmaceuticals, medical, aerospace and military equipment.

Currently, the USA has the most used currency in the world for international transactions and the world's foremost reserve currency, a transaction in US dollars of almost 38 trillion US dollars which accounts for 40% of all international transactions.

The expenditure on GDP

The US sends 3.5% of its GDP to the military which is accounted for 801 billion US dollars, R&D spending 3% of the American economy, spending on education 3%-3.5% of the GDP and spending on healthcare facilities almost 6.9% of the GDP.

Japan

Japan is an island country in East Asia the country is situated in the northwest Pacific Ocean and the population of the country is 12.50 Cr.

The expenditure on GDP

Japan's per capita income is 44,585 US dollars (GDP, PPP) and the country has a highly developed free market.

It is the third largest economy in the world and Its GDP is $5.06 trillion, japan's spending on R&D is approximately 3% of the total GDP of the country, currently, japan has no official army but still, the budget on self- defence Army is 1% of their GDP, spending on education is around 3% and on healthcare sector spending is around 10% of the GDP.

Germany

Germany is the second most populated country after Russia in Europe with a population of 83 million and the country is officially known as the Federal Republic of Germany, it is a sovereign state in central Europe and the country, shares borders with Denmark, Belgium, Luxembourg, Austria, in the east Czechia, Poland, Maritime border with Sweden and United Kingdom.

The expenditure on GDP

Germany is the fourth largest economy in the world after the USA, China and Japan. It has the largest nominal economy in Europe and fifth on the bases of PPP in the world.

The nominal GDP of Germany is 4.12 trillion US dollars and their per capita income is $50,802. Germany sending on Research and Development (R&D) is around 3% of Germany's GDP accounting for around 104 billion euros, spending on Healthcare almost 12.5%, on defence almost

2% and education almost 5% of GDP this is the bigger number than other leading country's GDP.

United Kingdom

The United Kingdom of Great Britain and Northern Ireland is known as the United Kingdom or Britain and the estimated population is 67 million. It is the fifth largest economy in the world, its GDP size is 2.67 trillion and its Per capita income is around $47,620.

The expenditure on GDP

United Kingdom's spending on education at 3.9% of GDP in 2018, on Research and Development (R&D), is 1.74%, on defence is around 2% and on Healthcare is around 8.4%.

India

India is the second highest populated country after China; it is one of the oldest civilisations and the country is Rich culturally.

As per data from the International Monetary Fund (IMF), India's Nominal GDP was around $3.4 trillion in 2021. It is the sixth largest economy in the world and based on purchasing power parity (PPP) third largest economy.

India is also one of the fastest-growing economies in the world, India's per capita is estimated in 2020 at almost $1,935 ranking 139th. As per the latest data, the nominal GDP is $2.66 trillion and purchasing power parity (PPP) is $8.66 trillion.

The expenditure on GDP

India is spending on their healthcare around 1.3% of GDP, on education around 3% to 3.5%, on research and development just 0.66% and on Defence 2.7% of GDP.

France

France is a European country and Paris is the capital city of the country, France has the largest exclusive economic zone in the world. It shares its border with Belgium, Luxembourg, Germany, Switzerland, Monaco, Italy, Andorra, and Spain in continental Europe, as well as Netherlands, Suriname and Brazil in the Americans via its overseas territories in French Guiana and Saint Martin collectively area of around 643,801 km2 and its total population approximately 67 million people as per 2021 data.

France retains its centuries-long status as a global centre of art, science and philosophy and France is also the world's leading tourist destination.

France is a developed country with the seventh-largest economy by nominal GDP and tenth-largest by PPP.

France was the first country to create an environment ministry in 1971; France was set to impose a carbon tax in 2009 at 17 euros per tonne of carbon emitted, which would have raised 4 billion euros of revenue annually.

The expenditure on GDP

France is spending on education 5.4% of GDP, on research and development 2.35%, on the military spending about 2% of GDP and healthcare facilities around 11%.

The total market size of glass manufacturing

The manufacturing market was estimated at $228.7 billion in 2020 and the growth of the market was a 4.1% compounded annual growth rate (CAGR) from 2021 to 2027.

It is estimated that the forecast market size of glass will be 330 billion approximately by end of 2027.

The growth and demand are proportionally parallel to each other by the year's demand of glass in the industries getting high including automobile industries, construction and other industries.

Glass is luxurious in use, it is generally decorative to the industry and for domestic use purposes apart from domestic use, and it is important to modern scientific advancement.

Majorly glass is using industries such as telecommunication, automobile, transportation, construction, electronics, medical and others.

USA and China are the major exporters, consumers and producers of glass there are many countries, that are doing the same and earning a lot of profit in figures but they have no concern for the environment, even though glass can be recyclable 100% without any loss of quality.

Glass recycling and solution (Futuristic Model)

What is glass?

Glass is very important for daily life; glass is inorganic material which is one of the largest producers in the industry. Glass is mainly made of sand, silicon dioxide (SIO2), limestone (calcium carbonate orCaCO3), sodium carbonate (Na2CO3) these are the main component of glass. The melting point of sand is 1700*C, it's important for glass manufacturing.

What is the recycling of glass?

Recycling is turning waste into useful material, recycling is known in general terms for the process of collecting and processing material, otherwise, it would have been thrown into the trash.

What are the Benefits of recycling?

But in recycling, we need fewer resources and we can reduce air pollution by 20% and water-related pollution by 50%.

Recycling will also help to reduce or clear the space occupied by the landfill which is filled with jars and bottles.

By recycling, we can minimize the unnecessary dumping of glass garbage into the landfill.

Energy cost will be less than about 2-3% for every 10% cullet used in the manufacturing process.

Recycling reduces emissions and consumption of raw materials that we have taken from nature

Recycling extends the life of manufacturing plants and equipment used for manufacturing glass.

Beer and soft drink bottles are getting recycled by almost 40%.

Recycling 1,000 tons can be creating over 8 jobs which can be a great initiative.

Recycling market in the world

As we all know recycling is the only way to solve the problem of waste because the total amount of glass produced globally is almost 209 million tonnes annually as per data for 2022 post-pandemic in the world.

Recycling of glass is very less than manufacturing by the industry every year; globally percentage of glass recycling is up to 50% when we include countries like China, America, Germany, France, India etc.

So adoption of recycling by the countries is necessary in this way the world energy, financially growth, and the environment can be saved.

The recycled glass market size was almost USD 3 billion in 2021 and its projected yearly growth rate is around 5.5%-

6% (compound annual growth rate), due to its benefit to the environment likewise: low energy consumption, low carbon dioxide emission etc. By the end of 2028 glass recycling industry size will be forecast to account for USD 4.5 billion.

New glass manufacturing is 209 million tonnes; comparatively to recycling glass is approximately 90 million tons, it is very necessary to increase the rate of recycling.

Total recycling of manufacturing on a country basis:

United States of America

In the USA glass is a major product for decoration they use, glass in construction, liquor bottles, packaging, car manufacturing, house windows and others.

The USA has one of the largest glass consumers and glass waste producers in the world as well, but when we see the glass waste management of the USA is not exemplary even though there should be more investment in this sector.

The glass generation in all production was 12.3 million tons, which was 4.2% of all waste management generation.

EPA combined data from the Glass Packaging Institute with information from state environmental agencies to measure the recycling of glass containers in the United States. The number of glass containers was 3.1 million tons in 2018, for a recycling rate of 31.3 per cent.

China

China is a manufacturing Hub of the world, it manufactures so many types of products such as electronic gadgets, home decorative products, hardware products, fashion accessories, beauty products, toys etc.

That's why China is known as a manufacturer of some products china is the largest manufacturer and exporter in the world. In glass exportation, china is holding the first position that is around the world's 24% of glass export.

Total manufacturing output of $4,865.82 billion in 2021(it was last calculated by experts).

China's glass recycling

Shanghai is one of the fourth direct administrative municipalities of the People's Republic of China, with a population of 25 million (approximately) as of 2021 shanghai's most populous Urban area of China generates 800,000 tons of glass waste annually.

China develop a group called "The Shanghai Group" that is a glass recycling firm in 2018, the firm was using an automatic optical sorting line and since they are trying to scale it up every single day, the firm can recycle 2 million tons of glass waste every year, the company was holding largest capacity worldwide.

The recycling method can save 800kg of quartz sand, 130kg of caustic soda, 130kg of limestone and 140 litres of heavy oil for 1 ton of glass packaging from that we can save high consumption of natural resources and minimize wastage.

There is no accurate data found for calculating the total recycling percentage of China but by the experts, it is almost 13% which is very lower than the manufacturing rate of new glass products.

India

In the 17th century, the kingdoms were investing in decorative items to popularize their fame and name. It was very luxurious, the varnished glass produced in Karnataka and Uttar Pradesh.

Since then India became one of the manufacturers in Asia, major three glass producer states in India:

Uttar Pradesh - 100 factories (Firozabad), other major centres Bahjoi, Naini, Hiranagau, Hathras, Sasni, Allahabad and Jaunpur.

West Bengal – Kolkata, Haora, Raniganj, Belgachiya, Belgharia, Belur and Asansol.

Maharashtra- Mumbai, Talegaon, Satara, Nagpur, Kolhapur.

India is one of the largest consumers of glass products in Asia accounted more than 21 million metric tons each year, but only 45% of glass waste recycles because of mismanagement and there are no proper collection centres.

Europe

Europe Union (EU) is a political and economic union of 27 member states that are located primarily in Europe. Europe generated a nominal gross domestic product (GDP) of around USD 17.1 trillion in 2021.

The countries are known for higher education rates and are rich in technologies, they have 5.8% of the world's population and the population of the European Union is 447.7 million.

European countries are equivalent to 9.78% of the world's population and the population density of Europe is almost 34 square per km when we see the European Environmental model is exemplary to the world.

The recent recycling percentage of waste in the European Union is 37.9% and the world's average waste recycling percentage is less than 20%, which is almost half of the European Union.

The total glass production in Europe is almost 40 million tonnes each year and European countries have the capacity of 80% collection of glass waste and around 74% glass recycling rate.

The highest recycling percentage holds in Germany which is more than 85%.

Rubber

The first rubber introduced in the modern era that is considered by the experts in 1736 was in France, after the century South America was one of the main sources of rubber used during much of the 19th century.

Because the early 20th century the development of the automobile industry was seeking demand for rubber, the main source of rubber raw material was rubber trees and the major exporter countries were South America and some African countries.

In the early 1900s, the Congo Free State in Africa played a significant role in rubber exportation to the world.

Rubber is globally recognised for its multiple uses in many industries such as tyre industries in automobiles, and some household applications.

There are mainly two types of rubber in the nature

Natural rubber

Synthetic rubber

Natural rubber

Natural rubber is latex and in the primary level that is found directly from the tree, latex is a sticky, milky and white colloid drawn off by making incisions in the bark and collecting the fluid in vessels and refining it into the rubber that is ready for commercial processing.

Synthetic rubber

This rubber product was firstly introduced in 1909 and rapidly synthetic rubber industry was booming. It is known as polymerizing isoprene and the total revenue generation is around USD 30 billion globally in 2020 and US itself

generates 32 million metric tons of rubber products annually.
It is consist of polymers of the organic compound isoprene with minor impurities of other organic compounds.

Global market size Rubber waste management industry –
The global rubber recycling market was around USD 1.04 billion in 2021 and its growth rate is around 10% (CAGR).
Rubber can take generally 50 to 80 years to decompose in the environment and the rubber releases most toxic elements into the environment.
It causes Air pollution, water pollution and land pollution.
Due to highly pollutant effluents, the reason pollution is getting high and demands of effluents higher to the industries which are harmful pollutants to the environment.

Change in human tendency is a Solution for future

The environment is an important factor for an individual, society and the whole ecosystem.
An ecosystem is the chain of environments balancing every single circumstance object or condition by which living and non-living elements are surrounded, the complexity of this structure is every single organism or an ecological depends on each other.
But every single day the greed for resources are getting bigger and bigger, now humans have forgotten that the resources of nature are limited to the survival of future generation.

Humans are responsible for preserving or safeguarding minerals and natural elements such as water, Air, land, forest and others.

But for a while avidity of the materialistic world is increasing so that humans are started to mess with nature and we have seen tremendously dangerous consequences like climate change.

Impact of climate change

We are seeing a negative impact on the climate worldwide, the climate change is affecting global temperature and precipitation patterns.

These kinds of effects are turning into environmental disastrous events such as forest fires, storms, heat waves, floods and hurricanes.

Causes of climate change

Human activities are the major cause of methane emission of greenhouse gases, it directly affects vegetation, animals and human health.

Primarily we are saying that climate change by burning fossil fuels like coal, gas and petroleum products.

Human mistakes caused greenhouse gases and emissions to continue to rise, as a result, the Earth is now about 1.1*c warmer than it was in the late 1800s.

How do preserve natural resources?

The only way as we mentioned before is recycling that way we can restructure economical dependency on decomposable material for the environment.

The global waste management market accounted for USD 1.61 trillion in previous years, which is equivalent to 2% of the world's total GDP.

The total calculation of the world GDP is around USD 95 trillion and it is very necessary for saving natural resources;

the countries should invest by a collaboration of the United Nations or any new build world level institutes which should bound to the countries for investing at least 10% of world GDP.

Increasing recycling waste can be a good economic model and it can be a big help to the environmental economy.

We are not saying these investments should be non - profitable but it is important to understand we should develop an environment-friendly economy to save nature.

The environment is not only a physical issue but also an economic and social issue; humans need to live their life with some essential elements.

The basic need of humans is food, and energy but other luxurious items are secondary.

"Primarily humans used to fulfil their basic needs then they might move to a luxury, but with time nature is not the priority in human lives rather luxury is, for that of the human race, nature had to pay the price".

Humans have a lot of capacity to create new products and can develop unnecessary products for their desire that is the reason behind today's environmental disasters are taken place because for at least 250 years humans created a lot of unnecessary consuming products.

"Luxurious material may be a symbol of richness but sometimes it's killing of nature."

There are so many products built by humans without thinking about the negative result on nature.

The whole problem is arisen by using high harmful product consumption, as we know that the market is run by people and their thinking patterns of mind and mindset can directly affect their lifestyle.

The Collective lifestyle of a human directly affects the environment and their climate pattern because when we release any waste and harmful products into nature the automatically environment try to balance, but a large number of unnecessary products and materials imbalanced the environment.

Nature or the environment tends to purify itself so human only needs to control their consumption of items (plastic materials, petroleum products etc.) and switch to natural material for their fulfilment.

"Environment economy is the mother of all economies; if we want to stabilize all the economies so create a road map to environment economy."

The road map of an environment-friendly economy

If the environment changes its tendency then it will be impossible to control by human capacity, so it is time to change humans' over-consuming nature, for oneself and the betterment of society.

It is very necessary to take initiative by the important section of society such as institutions like schools, colleges, research centres and others.

Environment education should be the core of education policy.

Environment-based business is also part of the way to solve the problem.

It is necessary for to industrialists come together and create an atmosphere of the ness that depends on the environment.

"It is very necessary that create environment-friendly economy and policies by the governments or world community."

"Life belongs to nature and nature belongs to earth so let's save the earth by saving the environment"

www.ingramcontent.com/pod-product-compliance
Lightning Source LLC
LaVergne TN
LVHW100338181026
850499LV00039B/1131
* 9 7 8 9 3 5 6 6 7 0 0 6 8 *